Exercises fo

&

Group Development

Building Blocks for Intimacy, Awareness & Community

Charles Bufe
&
Dale DeNunzio, Ph.D.

See Sharp Press ◆ Tucson, Arizona ◆ 1998

Bufe, Charles.
    Exercises for individual and group development / Charles Bufe
and Dale Denunzio -- Tucson, AZ : See Sharp Press, c1998.
    80 ; 22 cm.
    ISBN 1-884365-15-9
    1. Group relations training. 2. Group relations training -
Problems, exercises, etc. 3. Small groups. 4. Group games.
I. Denunzio, Dale. II. Title.

                    302.14

Cover Design by Clifford Harper. Interior design by Charles Bufe.
Interior typeset in Palatino. Cover typeset in Gill Sans.

Contents

Preface

Group work has become increasingly popular in recent years. It's become popular in professional circles, because there's convincing evidence that it's every bit as effective as individual therapy in treating many disorders; and it's become equally popular in nonprofessional circles, because of its obvious power—it allows gains in certain areas, such as intimacy and communication, that would be nearly impossible to achieve through individual work. And, because of its nature, it's a very valuable tool for those attempting to build community.

At the same time that interest in group work has skyrocketed, there's been a near-total lack of material on group exercises. Hence this manual. *Exercises for Individual and Group Development* is intended for both professional and lay facilitators. In it, we carefully describe nearly three dozen exercises of various types drawn from diverse sources (cognitive-behavioral therapy, gestalt, psychodrama, acting exercises, etc.). We include both physical and verbal exercises, trust-, intimacy-, and awareness-building exercises for beginning, intermediate, and advanced groups. We've facilitated and participated in virtually all of these exercises, and we trust that both lay and professional facilitators will find them of use in a great variety of group settings.

To facilitate ease of use, we've arranged the exercises in both the Verbal Exercises and Physical Exercises chapters in order, from those most suited to beginning groups to those suited only to advanced groups; we've mixed those suited to groups at any stage in with the exercises for beginning groups.

Finally, we intend to publish a revised and expanded edition of this manual in a few years, and we'd love to hear your feedback. We'd especially like to hear about exercises which went well, exercises which didn't, and any problems that you encountered during facilitation. We appreciate your input.*

—Charles Bufe & Dale DeNunzio, May 29, 1998

---

* Please contact us c/o See Sharp Press, P.O. Box 1731, Tucson, AZ 85702-1731, or at seesharp@earthlink.net

Groups

A group has a life of its own. It's important to recognize that a few simple decisions regarding its structure can help to maximize benefits and to promote depth of experience for its members. A group can provide benefits to its members that they cannot attain individually.

Closed groups, groups that do not admit new members during the life of the group, tend to move through four stages. (Please realize these stages are not always clear cut; and some members move through these phases at a different rate than other members.) The first stage is characterized by high enthusiasm, high expectations, and politeness. In this stage, members display varying levels of anxiety as they seek to fit into the group and to discover how the other members perceive them; they're also trying to see if the group can provide what they want. At this time, members of most groups will turn to a leader in the expectation that he or she will provide structure and direction.

This stage is often followed by a second one characterized by splintering, arguments, and power struggles. In this stage, there is often a discrepancy between what members experience inwardly and what they present to the group. Some call this phase "chaos." In it, the group's emphasis is on differences rather than similarities. Many groups dissolve during this stage, because members decide that the group is not worth the energy that they are putting into it.

If the group survives, this stage leads to a third one in which members look for ways in which they can peacefully agree and disagree. Members of a group at this phase have learned to tolerate differences, and can begin to find solutions to the group's difficulties. Finding norms, or establishing what will and won't be accepted by the group, occurs during this stage.

The fourth stage is one in which individuals genuinely work together in a cohesive, cooperative manner and accomplish more as a group than they could accomplish individually; and, often, the benefits to group members are benefits that they could not receive through any amount of individual effort. The group operates as a whole, and the whole is truly more than the sum of its parts.

❖   ❖   ❖

There are many different kinds of groups, and one of their fundamental distinguishing features is whether they are open or closed. Open groups allow the addition of new members throughout their existence. Because of this, open groups sometimes go through waves of the phases described above, with new people moving out-of-sync through these four stages, which can significantly affect the rest of the group. When this occurs, it's helpful for the facilitator to make note of it and to remind the group that newer members may be in a different place than everyone else, and that neither place is right or wrong.

The advantage of open groups is that they're less dependent upon the continued participation of members than closed groups, because if original members drop out, they can be replaced. The disadvantages of open groups are that they often sacrifice cohesion for flexibility, and that, because of the "wave" phenomenon, there is often a fairly high level of conflict in them.

Closed groups, of course, do not have to deal with this "wave" phenomenon, which reduces the level of conflict in them. As well, because everyone in a closed group will be at more or less the same stage (as outlined above), there is usually more cohesion in closed groups than in open groups, which allows for more risk-taking and "deeper" work. The primary disadvantage of closed groups is that they're highly dependent upon the continued participation of original members, and they can and do collapse if enough members withdraw.

Other issues that the facilitator and/or group need(s) to address are the lifetime of the group and the frequency of its meetings. Is the group open ended, with no predetermined duration, existing as long as its members care to meet? Or is the group set up from the start to be time-limited, with meeting dates known in advance? Both approaches have advantages and disadvantages. Some people like knowing that a group will meet for a limited time, and feel comfortable devoting their time and energy knowing that it will end at a specified time. Others like the idea of flexibility, participating without having to make agreements or commitments beyond the near future.

There are other questions. Will attendance be mandatory? Will attendance determine group membership? In other words, if a person misses a certain percentage or a certain number of meetings, will he or she be excluded from the group? We suggest that groups, especially time-limited groups, adopt this practice, because it prevents individuals from dropping in and out, which not only allows those individuals to avoid dealing with their own issues, but also tends to create tension by making it difficult for those who have issues with the drop-in members to address those issues in the group. As well, having drop-in members tends to produce a shallow level of trust, which is highly undesirable, especially in intimacy-building groups. In short, allowing members to freely drop in and out is disruptive. It makes it difficult to create the kind of safe atmosphere that allows people go deeply into their own issues and to achieve real intimacy. A time-limited, closed structure avoids this problem; it sends the message that conflict will be dealt with.

We suggest that all of these questions be addressed and answered prior to starting a group, and that they be considered in light of the group's purpose. To put these questions in more schematic form, and to add several more: How long will meetings be? How often will they be? Where? Will the group be open or closed? How many, if any, meetings will a member be allowed to miss before he or she is excluded? Will extenuating circumstances be considered? Will the group continue to exist if the facilitator leaves? And—the question that should be the first to be addressed—who decides these matters, the facilitator or the group members?

Finally, different individuals come to groups with different agendas and different expectations. It is helpful for a facilitator to be as clear as possible in the opening sessions about the intent of the group, and what the group is and is not. It is also helpful in the early stages of a group for the facilitator to elicit the group members' fears, concerns, and expectations. Being clear about all of these things will go a long way toward producing an effective, cohesive group.

Facilitation

Facilitators play a key role in intimacy-, awareness-, and community-building groups. The primary reasons for the existence of facilitators are:

1) To keep things running smoothly and on time;
2) To keep check-ins, discussions, and exercises on track;
3) To create a safe atmosphere;
4) To help individuals develop awareness of their issues;
5) To help them deal with their issues.

For all of these things to happen, it's necessary that facilitators be assertive and, often, directive. It's also very important that facilitators avoid the "niceness" trap—i.e., not asking tough or embarrassing questions when they're called for; not calling disruptive individuals on their behaviors; not starting meetings on time for fear of confronting socializers and latecomers; and letting disturbed, unclear persons run their patterns rather than confront them and deal with it. (In general, the more unclear a person dealing with issues is, the more active and directive the facilitator should be. Using a laid-back, nondirective approach with unclear people isn't helpful to them or to the group. Yes, you won't have to confront them, but you'll waste a lot of time, and you won't help them work through their issues—in fact, you'll help them stay stuck.)

Several things usually underlie these unfortunate behaviors by facilitators: 1) the fear of conflict, of not being thought "nice" by the group's members; 2) lack of self-confidence; and 3) uncertainty about how to deal with certain individuals and certain situations.

Regarding these stumbling blocks, niceness is probably the most insidious. As long as a facilitator is overly concerned about everyone in the group liking her or him, s/he won't be able to devote full attention to the issues or problems at hand. Instead, he or she will be focusing on appearance management—how others perceive her/him—and will be afraid to employ many effective techniques because they don't appear to be "nice." To put this another way, it's very important for a facilitator to be aware of his or her own issues, and to stay on top of them, if s/he's to be as grounded, helpful and objective as possible.

Lack of self-confidence is a real problem for many people, including therapists and other facilitators. While there's no magic formula for achieving self-confidence, it's usually the case that if you act as if you're self-confident, others will perceive you as being so, which will in turn reinforce your feelings of self-confidence. It's also helpful to facilitators to realize that most people are so concerned about their own issues and image that they are, in fact, paying much less attention to you than you imagine—even when you're in a highly visible role, such as that of facilitator.

Uncertainty about how to deal with issues or situations is also a problem at times for almost all facilitators. A key realization here is that, as long as your intent is good, no matter what you do, you probably won't make the situation worse than it already is; in other words, almost anything you try will be better than doing nothing or taking a nondirective approach (which is close to doing nothing).

Another important realization is that as long as you act as if you know how to deal with a problem, those having the problem will tend to have confidence in both you and in the process that you use—and they'll probably get something out of it simply because they have that confidence and allow themselves to go with it. Of course, it's not good to always attempt to bluff your way through unfamiliar situations, and for that reason it's good to get as much experience in groups —as participant and facilitator—as you possibly can; and it's also good to familiarize yourself with as many psychological techniques and theories as you possibly can, because different approaches work with different people.

Finally, knowing yourself—your issues, beliefs, trigger points, blind spots, etc.—is one of the best ways that you as a facilitator can make yourself helpful and effective. Self-awareness, whether gained through experience, through therapy, or through one's own desire to delve deeper into oneself, is a powerful and useful tool. Your facilitation will be most effective when you're as clear and self-aware as possible, and when you're as free from "attachments" (in other words, expectations of desired outcomes, or attractions or aversions to group members) as possible.

For example, being in any kind of a living, business, or romantic relationship with any group member impedes a facilitator's ability to be objective and clear when facilitating group processes. If a facilitator wants to pursue an attraction to a member, whether consciously or unconsciously, it is likely that this attachment will interfere with his or her effectiveness, and thus with the effectiveness of the group. An attraction/attachment may make it difficult in the group process for the facilitator to appropriately address issues or confront the person they're attracted to. If attraction, or any other attachment, arises, one of the best ways for a facilitator to handle it is to acknowledge the attachment to him or herself. And the best next step, if the attachment persists, is for the facilitator to acknowledge it to the group. This allows the members to give feedback to the facilitator, and it opens the way for discussion of the topic, which can help all group members deal with whatever issues or feelings they may have about the matter. It also models authenticity and openness.

Whether one has had much, some, or no group facilitating experience, self-awareness has tremendous value. Before you facilitate a group, it may be helpful to take time to ask yourself several questions, and to jot down your answers. (Writing down answers is almost always more helpful than merely answering questions in your head.) You might find the following questions of use in this regard:

- Do I have issues with either of my parents?
- What issues?
- What issues trigger my anger?
- What issues trigger my shame?
- How confident am I in social situations?
- What kinds of situations do I find difficult to deal with?
- How do I feel about authority?
- How do I deal with authority?
- How do I deal with people who disagree with me?
- How do I feel about criticism?
- How do I deal with people who challenge me?
- How do I deal with people in crisis?
- What are my attitudes on sexuality?
- On conformity?
- On race?
- On age?
- On economic status?

To gain greater personal insight, you might also find it useful to go through the "Personal Questions" exercise (pp. 30–35) and to write out your answers.

Physical Exercises

There are three basic types of physical (or body) exercises:
1) Icebreakers; 2) Trust builders; and 3) Intimacy builders.

Icebreakers

Icebreakers are physical exercises that normally last only
a few minutes and come at or near the start of a meeting.
Their reason for being is that they help people to loosen up,
and therefore help them give fuller attention to the following
discussions or verbal exercises than if they went into them
cold.

Trust Builders

Trust builders also often come near the start of a meeting.
In addition to helping to break the ice, they serve another
important function: they set the stage for exercises that
require trust, exercises that involve self-disclosure.

Intimacy Builders

Intimacy builders often follow icebreakers or trust-
building exercises, and often take up entire sessions by
themselves. They serve some of the same functions as ice-

breakers and trust builders, but they also serve to produce a type of physical comfort and easiness in a group not achievable through the other two types of physical exercises. Of course, not all groups will *want* such a level of physical easiness, but in many types of groups, such as community-building groups, it can be very helpful.

Icebreaking Exercises

Back Rubs

Size: Works best in groups of 10 or more—circle is too tight in smaller groups.

Time: 4 to 10 minutes.

Stage: Any stage, though especially useful for beginning or intermediate groups.

Contraindications: Overly aggressive or violent tendencies.

Have everyone stand and form a circle, facing each others' backs. Then tell them to give a shoulder massage to the person standing in front of them. Also tell them to let the person giving the back rub know if anything hurts. (Some people tend to get a bit carried away with this exercise, especially if they're not used to giving massages; others in the group may be hypersensitive to even a light massage touch.) After two to five minutes, tell them to stop, turn around, and give a shoulder massage to the person who was giving them one. Tell them to stop after they've spent the same amount of time giving/receiving massages in both directions.

Circular Knee Sits

Size: Works best in groups of 12 or more.
Time: About 2 minutes.
Stage: Beginning.
Contraindications: Obesity.

Have everyone face in the same direction, facing each others' backs, and form as tight a circle as possible. Then tell them to sit down. Some might be reluctant to do this, but if everyone sits down simultaneously, everyone will end up sitting comfortably on the knees of the person behind them. In this exercise, a 100-pound woman can comfortably support a 200-pound man on her knees. Overcoming the initial reluctance to sit and the surprise at the comfort of sitting are most of the fun in this exercise; the rest of the fun comes when people have to disengage. It's best not to do this exercise if you have extremely obese people in your group.

Unknotting

Size: 5 to 15 people; for larger groups, it's best to break up into two or more groups of up to 15.
Time: Takes about 3 to 10 minutes.
Stage: Beginning.
Contraindications: Physical disabilities such as arthritis and back problems.

Have the group form a circle, and have everyone in it extend their arms in front of them crossing their own hands, one over the other. Then instruct everyone to grab two hands at random, but not two hands from the same person. Next, tell them to unknot themselves. This will involve some people raising their joined hands over others, and some people lowering theirs so that others can step over them. When finished, the group should be in a circle again, though some folks will be facing in and others facing out. Sometimes the group will wind up in two or even three unconnected circles; it doesn't matter. If the group still isn't unknotted at the end of 5 minutes (this sometimes happens), end the exercise even though some folks will want to continue with it. (Others won't, and it's better to end it rather than to pressure them to continue in an exercise in which they've lost interest.)

Wink Game

Size: Works best in groups of 10 to 30
Time: 10 to 20 minutes
Stage: Any, but good for beginning groups.
Contraindications: Overly aggressive or violent tendencies
Remarks: Works best in sexually balanced groups, though
   strict sexual balance isn't necessary. For this exercise,
   there must be an even number of people in the group; sit
   out or participate yourself in order to make the number
   come out even.

Count how many people are in the group and arrange
half that many sturdy, armless chairs plus one in a loose
circle. Have half the group (men, if the group is sexually
balanced, or some of the men if there are more men than
women) sit in the chairs with the other half of the group
standing behind them, arms at sides. There will be one
empty chair with a person standing behind it. Instruct the
person behind the empty chair to wink at one of the sitters,
and for the sitter to try to jump up and try to go to the empty
chair before the person behind them can grab them by the
shoulders. Also instruct the sitters to sit back down if they
feel a solid grip on their shoulders, and not to struggle.
(Some people will have a tendency to do this unless
instructed not to.) When a sitter has successfully moved to
the previously empty chair, the person behind the newly
empty chair will wink at other sitters until one of them
successfully moves, etc., etc. After five to ten minutes, tell the
group that was standing to sit down, and tell the group that
was sitting to stand behind the chairs. Continue as described
above for another five to ten minutes.

What Do You Do?

Size: Done in pairs. Works with any even number of participants.
Time: 10 to 15 minutes.
Stage: Any, but good for beginning or intermediate.
Remarks: This useful exercise is jolts people out of often-unconscious ways of acting and speaking.

Pair off the people in your group, then have one person in each pair ask, "What do you do?" The other person answers (e.g., swim, fly, mop the floor, read a book, etc.), and the person who *asked* the question then pantomimes the action. The other person then asks, "What do you do?" and the person doing the pantomime stops and answers (drive, jump, have sex, etc.). The person who *asked* the question then pantomimes the answer, and so on. Normally the switching back and forth begins slowly and then gets faster and faster. After a predetermined time (10 or 15 minutes) end the exercise by loudly saying "Stop!"

How Do I Feel?

Size: Works in groups of any size.

Time: 5 to 10 minutes.

Stage: Any, but the more difficult variations (2 & 3) are probably better suited to intermediate and advanced groups than to beginning groups.

Remarks: There should be an even number of participants, so participate in or sit out this exercise yourself in order to make the number even. The purpose of this exercise is very similar to that of the "What do you do?" exercise —to jolt individuals out of their customary ways of thinking and acting. The first variation is relatively easy, but the second and third variations are more intense. Most group participants will flounder and, at least at first, will probably find these latter variations uncomfortable. So, the first time you do them, it's probably best to keep them brief. It's also a good idea to do another short icebreaker that your group finds comfortable.

Variation 1

Have your group members line up in two rows facing each other, about two feet apart. Then instruct the people in one of the rows to make an "I feel" statement about a feeling or physical state (for example, "I feel happy," "I feel sad," "I feel sick"; and the statement should be different for every person), and for those opposite them to express that feeling through body language. Have the row speaking make a new "I feel" statement roughly every 30 seconds. After three or four such statements, reverse the roles.

Variation 2

Have your group members line up in two rows facing each other, about two feet apart. Then instruct the people in one of the rows to start making "I feel" statements about a feeling or physical state and simultaneously to contradict those statements with their body language. Since most people are rather unaware of body language (at least consciously), it'll probably be necessary for you to demonstrate such a statement/nonverbal contradiction yourself. A good one is to stand up, tightly cross your arms across your chest, cross your legs and lock them tightly, one against the other, look down, and through clenched teeth say, "I feel very relaxed." After making your demonstration, have the people in one row attempt to make statements and nonverbally contradict them while the other row watches impassively. After a few minutes, reverse the process.

Variation 3

Have your group members line up in two rows facing each other, about two feet apart. Then instruct the people in one of the rows to make an "I" statement about a feeling or physical state (e.g., "I feel happy," "I feel sad," "I feel sick"), and tell those in the other row to express *the opposite* of that feeling through body language. Have the row speaking make a new "I feel" statement roughly every 30 seconds. After three or four such statements, reverse the roles.

(A very good resource for learning common body language movements is *Signals: How to Use Body Language for Power, Success and Love*, by Allan Peese. New York: Bantam Books, 1984.)

Trust-Building Exercises

Falling Backwards

Size: Works best in groups of 8 to 12. Minimum group size is 6. If more than are 12 present, break up into 2 [or more] smaller groups.
Time: About 2 minutes per person.
Stage: Beginning.
Remarks: A perennial favorite, probably *the* most popular group exercise.

Have the group form a fairly tight circle facing in. Arrange the members so that large and small persons are evenly distributed around the circle. Have one person step into the center, close his or her eyes, turn around in a circle several times with eyes closed, put his or her heels together with knees straight, and fall backwards. Those behind him or her will catch the person falling and will gently pass him or her around the circle, eventually placing her/him upright in the center. The person falling should keep their heels together and knees straight throughout this time. Repeat this process until everyone has been in the center.

Body Lifting

Size: 8 to 10.

Time: About 2 minutes per person.

Contraindications: Obesity or extreme differences in size of group members.

Stage: Any.

Remarks: This exercise is an extension of the Falling Backwards exercise, and is a lot of fun. There should be an even number of participants, though this isn't absolutely essential. This exercise should be done outdoors or in a room with at least a 10-foot ceiling, plenty of room to move around, and no loose rugs or other objects on the floor; don't attempt this exercise in a room with ceilings lower than 9 feet.

Have one person lie down on the floor, and have the others line up evenly on both sides of his or her body. The tallest, strongest folks should be on either side of the torso, and one person should be by the head. Have the two sides gently place their hands under the person and gradually lift him or her above their heads, with (and this is important) the person at the head supporting the head of the person being lifted. Then tell everyone to slowly walk clockwise in a circle. After they've made one or two complete circles, have them gently lower the person back to the floor. Repeat until everyone has been lifted. A variation suited for rooms with low ceilings is to only lift the person to waist level, to stand in place, and to gently rock the person for a minute or two before placing him or her back on the floor.

Body Catching

This is another extension of the Falling Backwards exercise, and those familiar with that exercise often use the sequence Falling Backwards/Body Lifting/Body Catching. It involves having a person stand on a table, chair, ledge, or counter top, then falling into the arms of the other participants. We do NOT recommend that you try this exercise, because it's physically riskier than the others, and even if no one involved is seriously hurt, it can be unpleasant for those doing the catching. Obviously, the greater the height the person falls from, the greater the impact. So, while we do not recommend this exercise under any circumstances, we especially do not recommend it when there is an elevation difference of more than two or three feet between the person falling and those doing the catching. Because we do not recommend this exercise, we are not including instructions for it. We mention it only because it's fairly popular, and because some of those reading this manual might be exposed to it in one or another group. If you are, and are invited to participate, we strongly urge you to decline.

Intimacy-Building Exercises

Eyes-Closed Touch

Size: Works best with groups of 12 or more.
Time: 10 to 30 minutes.
Stage: Beginning.
Contraindications: Sexism and/or sexually aggressive
tendencies.
Remarks: Primarily for intimacy-building groups.

Have everyone except you and perhaps one helper form
a loose circle, facing in. Tell the group, "Please close your
eyes and keep them closed. When the music starts, start to
walk toward the center very slowly. When you find other
people, touch them gently in any way that feels comfortable,
but do not touch them sexually. Stay as long as you like with
other people, but also feel free to move away as quickly as
you want or to pass them by. Start to move slowly inward as
soon as the music starts."

Start the music, and keep an eye on what's happening.
(Various types of "new age" Muzak® are good for this
exercise, as is some of the piano music of Debussy and Satie;
the important thing is that it be slow, soft, relaxing, and
nonvocal.) If people start to wander away, gently guide them
back toward the others. It's OK to participate yourself if
you're in a nonprofessional setting (and it's fun), but do look
up every moment or two to check out what's going on.

To end the exercise, gradually turn the music down and
then off, and tell everyone to open their eyes.

Group Massage

Size: Groups of 5.
Time: 15 to 20 minutes per person.
Stage: Intermediate or advanced groups, or for groups
formed specifically as massage groups.
Remarks: Best done nude, and works best in a well-heated
room. Primarily for intimacy-building groups. Because of
the intimate nature of this exercise, it's a good idea to give
people advance notice of it.

Use of massage oil is recommended, as are massage
tables. Allow 10 to 20 minutes per person, though it's OK
to go longer if participants decide to; but we don't
recommend that, especially in groups larger than five,
because people's hands tire. It's essential that you start at
least close to on time, and it's very desirable that latecomers leave rather than join in. It's a good idea to have
a potluck and/or schmoozing session first in order to help
people loosen up.

Since massage oil will probably be used, it's best to do
this exercise on pillows or cushions covered with sheets
of plastic, or with old sheets or towels that you don't care
about staining if massage tables are unavailable. While
massage tables are preferable to cushions or pillows,
we've assumed that most groups will not have access to
massage tables, so we've written the instructions for those
without them. If you have massage tables, substitute the
word "stand" for "kneel" and "massage table" for "pillows or cushions" in the following instructions.)

Begin by telling everyone that this exercise is clothing
optional, and that anyone uncomfortable with nudity should
leave. Also tell them that they should undress to the extent

that they feel comfortable. Also emphasize that this is a sensual, not a sexual, massage, and that those involved should behave accordingly. Because you'll want all of the groups to finish more or less at the same time, it's a very good idea to get group agreement about the time per massage before you start; and rather than ask the members of the group how long they want to go, it's better (at least much easier and quicker) to say, "We normally spend about 15 minutes on each person. Is everybody OK with this?" Allow a couple of minutes for those so inclined to undress, and for those uncomfortable to leave, and then split up into groups of five. (Counting off isn't a bad idea; and if you don't come up with an exact multiple of five, it's OK to have some groups of five and some groups of six; a group of seven will also work.)

One person in the group should lie face down on pillows or cushions, and the others should line up kneeling two on each side. If there's a sixth person, s/he should kneel by the head; and if there's a seventh, s/he should kneel by the feet. Everyone giving the massage (except the person doing the head, if there is such a person) should rub a little massage oil on their hands. (Never drop cold massage oil directly on the person being massaged.) One person should lead the massage, and the others follow his/her strokes and movements. The effect should be that of giving a massage with one gigantic pair of hands. If there is a sixth or seventh person, they should massage, respectively, the head and feet of the person being massaged, independently of what the people on either side are doing. The person leading the massage should be experienced at giving massages and should know a wide variety of strokes, though novices can learn fairly quickly from observation and should be able to lead this exercise after participating in it a few times. When the time limit (we suggest 15 minutes) is reached, end the massage.

(It's a good idea to keep a clock in sight, so that everyone gets more or less the same amount of time.) Then take a break of perhaps five minutes so that everyone can wash their hands and so that the person who was massaged has time to come back to earth. After the last person in your group is through, relax and wait for the other groups to finish (unless, of course, you're the last to finish). Thank everyone for coming, and have a closing circle if you wish.

Verbal Exercises

Appreciations

Size: 15 or fewer.
Time: 2 to 20 minutes.
Stage: Useful at any stage.
Remarks: This exercise is often done at the end of group sessions. It's especially useful when difficulties or interpersonal frictions have arisen during a session.

There are many variations on this exercise. One of the easiest is having have your group form a circle, and then, in turn, having everyone tell the person to their right something that they like or appreciate about them. After everyone has done this, reverse direction and have everyone tell the person on their left something that they like or appreciate about them. Do this one appreciation at a time, so that everyone in the group can hear what everyone else says.

A variation is to have one person sit in the center receiving appreciations from everyone else in the group. This can be a very powerful experience for shy individuals and other persons with self-image problems. After doing this version of the exercise, it can be useful to briefly hear the reactions of the person in the center to being appreciated and to being the center of attention and, perhaps, to question him or her about those reactions.

A third variation is to use this as a closing exercise. Here, you form a tight circle facing inward, and have everyone tell the person directly opposite them one thing that they appreciate about them.

A final variation is to form a circle and to ask anyone who feels moved to do so to give an appreciation of someone else in the group.

Questions (one-person focus)

Time: 10 to 15 minutes per person.
Size: Works best with groups of 5 to 7.
Stage: Any stage, but especially useful for beginning groups.
Remarks: This exercise is well suited to beginning groups, because it's a good way for people to get to know each other quickly, and because it's enjoyable and, usually, relaxing. Because verbose and domineering individuals tend to monopolize the floor in this exercise, it's generally necessary for facilitators to closely monitor them in order that all participants have a chance to ask questions.

Explain the exercise as follows: "We'll split into small groups in a few minutes. When we do, one person in each group will be the focus of attention for 15 minutes. The other people should ask that person anything that they genuinely want to know about him or her. Don't be afraid to ask hard or embarrassing questions. Just keep the focus on the person being questioned. Ask him or her about anything that you genuinely want to know, but please don't ask more than two questions in a row. The person being asked has the right to answer or to refuse to answer any question. After their 15 minutes are up, someone else will be the focus of attention. Keep going until everyone has gotten their 15 minutes of attention."

Then, depending on how many people there are, have everyone count off into groups of five, six, or seven, and tell the individual small groups where to meet. Toward the end of the exercise, check on the individual groups, and as soon as they're all done, have them all reconvene as a whole, and have a brief discussion of the exercise.

Personal Questions

Size: Groups of 2 to 4.

Time: Allow half an hour to an hour per person per set of questions.

Stage: Good for all stages, but especially for beginning groups

Remarks: It can take several sessions to get through all of these lists of questions. And it's a good idea to have group members write out their answers as homework.

Have your group count off into groups of two, three, or four, and give everyone a photocopy of one of the following sets of questions. Each person in the group will answer all of the questions. They can either take one question at a time and answer it in turn, or one person can answer all of the questions, then the next person can, etc.—it really doesn't matter; the important thing is that everyone answers all of the questions.

The Self

1) How intense is your love of life? Do you enjoy life now more than you did 10 years ago? 20 years ago? If not, why not, and what can you do to change that?
2) What do you not take responsibility for in your life? What are you going to do about it?
3) Do you underplan or overplan your life? Is there space for creativity and the unexpected?
4) Do you have a clear focus and purpose in life, or are you unfocused and purposeless?
5) Are you prepared to speak the unspeakable if you feel it is right to do so? Are you afraid to ask embarrassing

questions even if you have a legitimate reason for doing so? Do you sit on your thoughts for fear of offending others or because you want to be thought nice?

6) How clear are you about your agreements? Do you honor them? Do you have unspoken agreements with others that need to be out in the open?

7) To what extent can you laugh about yourself? About anything? Do you allow enough humor into your life? Do you allow too much humor into your life? Do you use humor to avoid taking yourself, and anything else, seriously?

8) To what extent do you judge your life through the eyes of your parents?

9) How often do you try to fit in in order to be liked? Do you do things you really don't want to do in order to influence others to like you?

10) Do you see and appreciate beauty around you and in yourself? If not, what is keeping you from seeing and appreciating it?

11) Do you have enough creative activities in your life? Are there creative things that you've been wanting to do but never have done?

12) What is your finest vision of yourself in the future? Where are you? How are you? What are your most important qualities? What are you doing? What is your purpose in life?

13) Do you make your dreams and desires real, or do they remain daydreams? What, if anything, do you need to change in order to realize your desires?

Philosophy/Beliefs

1) Do you have a spiritual or philosophical path that you follow in a committed way? What is it?

2) How open are you to new ideas? Do you seek out new knowledge and really listen to others? If not, do you want to change this, and if so, how?

3) Do you critically evaluate ideas and beliefs, or do you choose to "believe" things simply because they appeal to you? When the facts indicate that ideas that you dislike are correct, do you accept those disliked ideas or do you cling to your old ideas? If so, do you want to change this?

4) Do you "automatically" (without critical examination) accept the beliefs of any individual, organization, or text as true? If so, why? And do you consider this healthy?

5) Are there "isms"—ideologies, belief systems—in your life that you do not want to question? (For example, feminism, socialism, capitalism, christianity, vegetarianism, etc.) If so, what are they? If the premises opposite those of your favorite "isms" were true, how would that affect your life? What changes would you make?

6) What are your fundamental values? How do you express them in your daily life?

7) Do you believe in human freedom? If so, what does it mean to you? How do you express your respect (or lack of it) for freedom in daily and social life?

8) Under what, if any, circumstances is it justifiable for an individual to coerce, imprison, or kill another individual? Under what, if any, circumstances is it justifiable for the government to do these things?

9) Do you believe that you create your own reality? If you do, do you believe this absolutely? If so, how do you account for things such as murder, rape, poverty, and starvation?

10) Do you believe that you're a victim of circumstance and have little or no control over your own life? If so, why did you choose to participate in this group?

11) If you believe that you're neither entirely in control of your own reality nor entirely a victim of circumstance, what things do you have control over and what things do you not have control over? And are you really sure about these things, or do you place them in one category or the other because it makes it easier to (not) deal with them?

The Physical

1) What condition is your body in? Can you really do what you want with it? Is there anything that you've always wanted to do physically but never have?
2) What do you do that is harmful to your body? What *can* you do about it? What are you actually going to *do* about it?
3) What do you do that is healthy for your body? What *can* you do to become healthier? What will you actually *do* to become healthier?
4) Do you have the physical wellbeing that you want? Do you get as much sleep, food, sex, and relaxation as you want? If not, why not? And what can you do about it?
5) What is your physical state during peaceful, blissful moments?
6) What is your physical state during stressful moments?
7) Which state are you in more often?
8) What do you like about your body?
9) What would you like to change about your body? What, if anything, can you do to make the changes you desire? Why haven't you done so already? And are you really going to do anything?

The Emotions

1) How aware are you of your emotions? Identify the emotions that you feel or have felt.
2) How do you express your emotions? When, where, and why do you not show your emotions?
3) What are the easiest emotions for you to show? What are the hardest emotions for you to show? What can you do to make it easier to display them?
4) Do you frequently judge or condemn yourself? If so, how does this make you feel?
5) Do you moralistically judge others? If so, why? How does it make you feel? What are the personal and social consequences of judging others? Do you want to continue to do it?
6) What attracts you to others emotionally? What turns you off in others?
7) Do you blame others for your problems? Do you blame society, your partner, your friends, your co-workers, your children, your parents, the past? How much are these things really to blame for your problems?
8) What do you fear? How grounded in reality are these fears?
9) When was the last time you followed your impulses simply because it was fun to do so?
10) What makes you happy? What can you do to become happier?
11) Is your happiness dependent upon other people? If you're not happy now, do you believe that someone else must change, or do something, in order for you to be happy? Do you really want to wait for them to change or to act?

Sexuality and Love

1) What turns you on sexually? What turns you off? What attracts you to others sexually?
2) In sex, do you do the things that you really want to do? And do you do things that you don't want to do in order to please your partner(s)?
3) How easy is it for you to ask for what you want in sex?
4) Do you have any sexual desires that you've never stated? If so, what are they, and why haven't you stated them?
5) Are your emotions integrated into your sex life? And is sex integrated into your emotional life, that is, do you allow contacts of the heart to become sexual?
6) Do you have sexual fantasies that you have not yet realized? If so, what are they, and do you really want to realize them? If you do, what are you going to do about it?
7) Are you embarrassed by your sexual fantasies? If so, why?
8) How would you raise children to help them avoid sexual guilt and shame? What would you need to change in order to do that (if you had children)?
9) Do you need a relationship to feel complete? Do you feel you need a soul mate to be happy?
10) Do you find it easy or difficult to tell others that you're attracted to them? If it's difficult, why?
11) Do you avoid approaching others for fear of rejection? If so, do you want to change that? What will you do to change that?
12) Do you wait for others to approach you? If so, why? And do you consider this healthy?
13) What is your ideal vision of what a sexual relationship could be?

Who Are You?

Size: Works with almost any number of people, but the number should be even; so, participate yourself or sit it out in order to make the number even.

Time: As short as 20 minutes or as long as several hours, though 20 to 40 minutes is about average.

Stage: Any stage, but good for beginning groups.

Remarks: This is an excellent exercise to use in beginning groups and in open groups when newcomers are present. As well, if certain issues or tensions have arisen in a group, it can be useful to do this exercise while tailoring the questions to those issues or tensions. If you do this, though, you'll need to take care not to appear to be singling anyone out.

Have people line up in two rows sitting cross-legged with knees touching the knees of the person directly across from them. Instruct them: "Please remain seated with knees touching, looking directly into each other's eyes. One row of you will ask the person opposite you in the other row a question, and then just sit there, looking at them. You should show no physical reaction and say nothing. The people answering the question should talk nonstop for five minutes. I'll let you know when five minutes are up. The important thing is to keep talking. Don't stop. You don't even need to be honest or to make sense. Just keep talking. If you find that you're stuck and can't think of a thing to say, talk about being stuck and not being able to think of a thing to say. If you keep talking, eventually something else will come to you. Ready? The row with their back to me (the window, the wall, etc.) will now ask the row facing me, 'Who are you?'" (or any of the other questions listed below, or in the "Personal Questions" exercise, or any that you make up yourself). Then, if you're not participating, walk around observing the people doing the exercise and remind individuals, if needed, to keep on talking and/or not to respond in any way.

Time this exercise down to the second, and at the end of five minutes loudly say "Stop!" Ask the row that was listening to say, "thank you," and have the row that was talking ask the previously listening row the exact same question they were asked. Again, after five minutes, tell them "Stop!" and have the listeners thank the talkers. Then, before the next question, have one row remain stationary and the other row move one place to the right (or left—the important thing is that participants have different partners for each question). The person on the end of the moving row will need to go to the other end of the row.

In new groups and open groups with new members, it's generally a good idea to set aside a few minutes for participants to talk about their reactions to this game. It's also worth noting that this game can be done over and over; the list of useful questions is virtually endless.

Here are a few helpful questions to use during this game:

- Who are you?
- What do you want?
- What are you doing to get what you want?
- How do you stop yourself from getting what you want?
- Who am I?
- Why shouldn't you change?
- What do you fear?
- Who do you fear?
- What are you afraid to do?
- What is your highest vision of yourself?
- Where do you see yourself 10 years from now?

- What do you like about yourself?
- What do you do that harms yourself?
- What do you find hard to do, and why?
- What would you like to change in your behavior?
- What disgusts you? Why?
- What do you need to be happy?
- What do you want in a relationship?
- Tell me some big, fat lies.
- Sing me a song.
- Talk in someone else's voice.
- What do you want in life, and why?
- What does love mean to you? And how do you express it in your life?
- Who do you love, and why?
- What would you like to change in yourself?

Many of the questions in the "Personal Questions" exercise (pp. 30–35) are also appropriate for this exercise.

Vision Sharing

Size: Works well with groups of 4 to 6. If more are present, break into groups of 4 to 6.

Time: A minimum of 5 and a maximum of 10 minutes per person.

Stage: Useful for any group, but especially for beginning groups.

Remarks: This exercise is very helpful in clarifying goals and values. It's also useful in that it helps individuals get to know each other quickly. It's generally a good idea to set aside a few minutes after this exercise to talk about how participants liked the exercise, and if anything came up in their groups that they want to talk about more.

Explain this exercise to your group as follows: "We're going to break into small groups to let each other know what our highest visions are of ourselves, and what are goals are. The way it works is that one person will start talking and will continue until someone else raises their hand and starts to talk. Raise your hand if you're getting bored or have something that you want to say; but don't raise your hand if you just want to rescue someone. Also, there's no crosstalk in this exercise. Don't ask each other questions or make comments while someone else is talking. Any questions? OK, let's count off into groups of five (or four, or six) and get started."

At the end of the exercise, loudly say, "Stop!"

Luck of the Draw

Size: Works well with almost any number of participants.
Time: 30 to 60 minutes.
Stage: Beginning.
Remarks: The only limitation is that the number of participants be even, so sit out or participate yourself in order to
make the number even. The purpose of this exercise to is
help people get better acquainted. In beginning groups, it
can be done several times to good effect.

Have all of the people present write down their names on
pieces of paper and put them into a bowl or a hat. Mix them
well, and then draw out two at a time. The two people
whose names were drawn will now spend half an hour or an
hour (specify which—it'll be the same for everyone) doing
whatever they mutually agree to do. After the exercise is
over, it can be useful to briefly meet as a group, and for those
who wish to share to mention anything interesting or
unusual that they did or that they found out about each
other.

Fishbowl

Size: At least 4 women and 4 men—more are better.
Time: 3 hours.
Stage: Any.
Remarks: A very good exercise for gaining greater understanding of gender issues. Because the number of gender issues is so high, this exercise can be done several times by a group, though it's probably best to intersperse fishbowls with other exercises and activities so as not to burn out on them.

A fishbowl consists of men's group and women's group discussion meetings, but with a difference: The men (or women) sit in a close circle, with the members of the opposite sex sitting silently in a larger circle two or three feet behind them. Those in the inner circle then discuss for an hour specific gender-related questions, such as, "What makes a good lover?", "What do you like about the opposite sex?", and "What do you dislike about the opposite sex?" Those in the outer circle merely sit and listen. After an hour, the seating positions and roles are reversed. Finally, the men and women can meet together to discuss what they heard, and/or they can meet separately to discuss what they've learned about each other.

Potluck Questions

Size: 3 to 30.
Time: 60 to 90 minutes.
Stage: Any stage, though good for beginning groups.
Remarks: This game is an exercise in transparency. It's fun, though it can sometimes push people's buttons. If there are relatively few people, its good to have multiple questions for every individual. To keep things light, it's also a good idea to have a mix of serious and whimsical questions.

In advance, (you, the facilitator[s]) write at least one question, preferably two or three, per participant on separate pieces of paper. After writing out the questions, fold the papers in half and put them in an open box. When the session starts, one person takes a question, then answers it, then another person takes one, answers it, and so on, taking no more than three minutes per question (time them).
Some possible questions are:

- If you had $10 million, how would you use it?
- If you were God, what would you change in the world?
- If you woke up one morning and discovered that you were a member of the opposite sex, what would you do?
- What are you not?
- Are you attracted to anyone here, but haven't told them? And if so, who is it?

The questions from the "Who Are You?" (pp. 36–38) and "Personal Questions" exercises (pp. 30–35) can be used here, as can virtually any others that you come up with.

Group Creativity

Size: 3 to 20.
Time: At least one full group session.
Stage: Any, though good for beginning groups.
Remarks: This exercise is particularly helpful for bringing a
  group together. We recommend that the group choose a
  reasonably easy project so that the exercise results in a
  feeling of success rather than failure, due to unrealistically
  high expectations. It's best to get agreement by members
  on the type of project. This will help them to become
  invested in it, and will likely prevent them from blaming
  you if it doesn't work out the way that they want it to.

Tell the group members that they are going to work
together on a creative project. Mention several possibilities:
a photograph, a poem, a song, a collage, or even a service
project; and then add that it can be something entirely
different, if they so choose. Allow enough discussion time
(say 15 minutes) for the group to reach an agreement about
the type of project, how much time they, as a group, are
willing to allot to it, and what individual members are
willing to do. Once the parameters have been set, assemble
(or have the group assemble) all of the materials and tools
needed for the project, and encourage the group's efforts. It
is your responsibility to make sure that all members participate and that the group adheres to its agreements about time
and participation.

Note: It's often necessary to schedule the actual project for a
later date if the group decides upon an activity requiring
special materials, such as painting. But no matter what the
project, this exercise can produce great satisfaction among

group members, because it shows what the group is capable of when its members decide to work cooperatively, and each member can feel satisfaction with his or her contribution.

Symbols

Size: 5 to 12.

Time: Allow 5 to 10 minutes per person.

State: Any, but good for beginning groups after a few meetings.

Remarks: This is a light, enjoyable way for group members to get to know one another.

At the meeting prior to the one in which the exercise will be done, give all members a large paper bag and a list of questions:

1) What is a quality that you like in yourself?
2) What is a quality that you dislike in yourself?
3) What is a quality that you'd like to improve in yourself?
4) What is a quality that you hope others notice in you?

In the time between meetings, everyone will put items in their bags that symbolically answer the questions. For example, if someone is financially irresponsible and dislikes it, they might choose a bounced check to represent this, or if they like their playful side, they might choose a volleyball.

At the meeting, have everyone places their bags in one spot, and then mix them up. Have one member start by picking a bag and going through its objects for a few moments. (If a person picks their own bag, have them put it back and then mix up the bags again.) After the person finishes going through the objects, have them announce what they think each object represents and whose bag they think it is. Then, the person whose bag it was identifies him or herself and explains what each object represents. Then, that person chooses another bag, and the process repeats until all of the bags have been opened.

Truth or Consequence?

Size: 10 to 30.

Time: 1 to 2 hours.

Stage: Any stage, though best in groups that have met at least a few times and in which members feel comfortable with each other.

Remarks: A common children's game that can be a lot of fun, and a very useful exercise in transparency. Best done when people are relaxed, for example on social occasions after hot tubbing or saunaing or, at the least, after doing some kind of physical icebreaker. We also recommend that this be done in comfortable surroundings.

To start, ask one of the group members, "Truth or Consequence?" If the person says "truth," ask them a question, which they *must* answer truthfully. The question can be about *anything*—e.g., "What's your favorite book?", "What do you like and dislike about yourself?", "What do you think of me?", "Who are you most attracted to in the group?", etc. After answering, that person then asks someone else, of their choosing, "Truth or Consequence?" and the game continues.

If the answer was "consequence," the person answering must then do whatever the person who asked the question tells them to do (within reason, of course). Typically, the consequence is something like, "Make up and sing a song about [fill in the blank]," "Stand on your head," "Make a speech about [fill in the blank] while lisping," etc. The person does the "consequence" and then asks someone else, "Truth or Consequence?" and so on.

The game ends after a preset time, or whenever you (the facilitator) decide to end it.

Group Wishes

Size: Works with any size group, though it works best in groups of 5 to 10; if your group is much larger than 10, have people count off and break it up into smaller groups.
Time: 2 to 3 hours.
Stage: Any stage, though probably best for beginning and intermediate groups.
Remarks: This exercise is good for getting people to ask for what they want, and for making transparent the process of deciding whether or not to accede to the wishes of others. The number of wishes per person will depend upon the size of the group and the time allotted.

Start by having your group sit in a circle, hand out writing paper and pencils, and say, "We're all going to make two (or three, or four) wishes tonight. We're all going to ask the group, or other people in the group, for two (or three, or four) things that we want, and that we think the group or individual people in it can give to us or do for us here tonight during meeting time. Those asked can grant the wish or refuse it. Let's all think for a few minutes about what we want to ask for, and then write down our wishes."

After five minutes or so, ask the person to your right to recite their wishes. Those asked to do, or for, something will write it down, but not respond immediately. Continue this process until everyone has stated her or his wishes. Then, ask for a vote on any wishes addressed to the entire group. Don't discuss group requests—just vote—as discussion would eat up too much time. For the group as a whole to grant a wish, everyone must agree to it. Then go around in a circle again, asking each individual if he or she will grant the wishes addressed to them personally, and if so, why, and if not, why not. Finally, spend the rest of the meeting time fulfilling granted wishes, fulfilling any granted group wishes first. If time runs out before all granted wishes have been fulfilled, continue at the next scheduled meeting.

Note: A slightly higher-stakes version of this exercise is to have the asking and granting/denying take place during a meeting, but to have the fulfilling take place away from the meeting and at times agreeable to the askers and granters. This allows more elaborate and more personal wishes to be expressed and granted than is possible during a meeting.

Conflict Resolution

Size: The conflicting parties and 1 or 2 facilitators.

Time: Will vary, but it's good to set a time limit of no more than 2 hours.

Stage: Any.

Remarks: It's not good to have more than two facilitators, as if you have more things will tend to get chaotic. The time necessary for successful conflict resolution will vary tremendously. Strictly speaking, this isn't an exercise; but it can be a very intense verbal process, and members of the group who are not directly involved can observe and learn from it, so it's included in this section. There are many different styles of conflict resolution. The following style attempts not only to deal with the immediate conflict, but to also get at the underlying emotional issues.

Start by having the conflicting parties sit in chairs next to each other, at perhaps a 90 degree angle, but not directly facing each other (too confrontational). Next, ask them, one at a time, to state the problem in three minutes or less (time them) using "I" language, to avoid "you made me feel" and "it made me feel" statements, and not to interrupt each other. (The point is to get them to accept responsibility for their own emotions and to defuse hostility.) After each is finished speaking, ask the other to repeat what was said. Sometimes they'll repeat each other's statements accurately; sometimes they won't. When this happens, point out the inaccuracies and ask the misquoted person to repeat whatever was inaccurately stated. Then ask the other person to repeat it again. Do this until the statements are in agreement. This may take a few rounds, which is OK.

Next, question both parties individually about their feelings about the dispute and about the other person. Useful questions can include, "How do you feel toward [the other person]?", "Does your reaction remind you of reactions you've had to others, especially to your parents?", "Is [the other person] doing/saying things that you don't give yourself permission to do or to say and that you judge as wrong?" and "What are you afraid of losing or what are you afraid that you won't get because of [the other person's] behavior?"

The point of all of this is to get to and to deal with the underlying emotions rather than the surface conflict. Probably the most important thing for facilitators to remember in this process is to ask, not tell. If you think you've figured out what's going on and can lead a person to draw the appropriate conclusions through questioning, they are much more likely to accept those conclusions than if you simply told them, "Here's what's going on, and here's what you're doing."

The reason for this emphasis on dealing with the underlying emotions is that once they're dealt with, the surface conflict generally becomes easier to resolve. After the individuals have dealt with their emotions, it's appropriate to go on to simple conflict solving, to attempt to help both parties work out a win-win situation. And at that point, but not before, suggested solutions to the surface conflict are in order—but only after giving the conflicting parties time to come up with their own.

Note: This process won't always get at the underlying emotions. When that happens, it's wise to give up attempting to do so after a time, and to go on to simple problem solving. That is, simply ask both parties (repeatedly if necessary) what they want; then, after that's clear, attempt to help them find a compromise that they can live with.

Forum

Size: 3 to 50.

Time: 60 or 90 minutes.

Stage: Any.

Remarks: This is a process used at the ZEGG community in Germany. It bears no relationship to "The Forum," which is an offshoot of the Est cult.

This process is so multi-faceted that it's difficult to capture it in words. It's basically a form of psychodrama, and it's used primarily for the purposes of clarifying issues and for emotional processing. For this process to work best, an experienced facilitator is necessary. There is normally one facilitator, though sometimes there are also one or two assistant facilitators. Forums are normally called when something is "up" with one or more persons in a group, and they are normally called for specific reasons, though they can be called at scheduled times simply to deal with whatever arises. Facilitation is normally very directive in this process. The one drawback to "Forum" is that its success is highly dependent upon the skill of the facilitator(s).

Have everyone sit down in a circle around a large open space. When everyone is seated, the facilitator will ask if anyone wants to speak first. The first person to speak rises and begins to walk around the interior of the circle, stating whatever is on his or her mind. Normally, the person will continue to walk; and if he or she stops, the facilitator will prod him or her to continue walking. The facilitator will often encourage the person to act out, often exaggeratedly, whatever it is they're talking about, and will sometimes give specific directions about that acting out. (For example, if a person was complaining about the unfairness of life, the facilitator might instruct them to walk bent over, as if they were carrying the weight of the world.) The facilitator will also often ask the person questions to clarify matters or to bring out underlying issues, may ask the person in the center to role play (as in becoming one of their parents), and will sometimes participate in the role playing him or herself. The facilitator determines when the person in the center sits down. If the person is just rambling to no point, the facilitator will sometimes tell them to sit down; and at other times the facilitator will keep them up longer than they want, if he or she senses that there are unaddressed issues. After the first person sits down, there is a pause of at least three breaths before the next person gets up (anyone can get up if they feel moved to do so), and so on. During this process, those sitting in the circle remain silent, participating only if asked to do so by the facilitator.

There are several rules in the forum process. Some are:

1) The person in the middle should, normally, walk around and follow the facilitator's instructions.
2) That person should never sit down or stand motionless in the center unless directed to do so by the facilitator.
3) Those in the circle should participate only if directed to do so by the facilitator.
4) Only one person is normally up in the center at any time, unless the facilitator instructs someone else to also get up.
5) If the person in the center is addressing someone in the circle, s/he should *not* look directly at that person when addressing them, but instead should look at someone else in the circle, or at an inanimate object.
6) Those sitting in the circle should remain silent and should not direct questions or comments to the person in the middle.

7) There should be a short pause between the time one person sits down and the next gets up.

8) The person in the middle should not touch or grab the facilitator, unless instructed to do so, but it's OK for the facilitator to touch the person in the middle.

9) Those at a forum should look at themselves, other people and their issues as impersonally and nonjudgmentally as possible. That is, rather than being enmeshed in their emotions, they should attempt to look at themselves and others as "case studies," to attempt to "look down from above" on what's going on rather than to look at it "horizontally," that is, emotionally/subjectively.

10) Forums are normally held for specified amounts of time (usually 60 or 90 minutes), but there is some flexibility in their length. Often a forum will come to an obvious stopping point, and the facilitator will normally end it at that time.

A few words of caution are in order here: The forum process is more dependent upon the skill of the facilitator than any other exercise or procedure described in this manual. In the hands of a skilled facilitator, a forum can be amazingly effective and transformative; but in the hands of an unskilled facilitator, it can be boring and useless.

As well, don't expect to work through issues *during* a forum. The forum process is useful for getting issues out on the table and for making them clear. Resolution—if it occurs —normally takes place sometime *after* the conclusion of a forum. (You should tell this to the participants before the forum begins.)

ABCs

Size: Done in groups of any size, but generally with one participant and one facilitator, and with the rest of the group observing.

Time: Normally about 5 to 10 minutes per person.

Stage: Any.

Remarks: This is a standard Rational Emotive Behavior Therapy (REBT) exercise. It can be done either individually or in a group setting, though it's probably most useful to teach it in a group setting because participants learn from each other's examples. There are two purposes to this exercise: to help individuals become aware of how their thoughts determine their emotions; and to help them learn to change their emotions.

One important thing to remember when facilitating this exercise is that negative, unhappiness- or anger-causing emotions are virtually always triggered by absolutistic beliefs, which usually appear in self-talk as "must" or "should" statements. Therefore, when facilitating this exercise, look for the "musts" and "shoulds."

Finally, this is, in part, a *written* exercise. It's extremely important that you do this exercise using a blackboard or large drawing pad (and magic marker), on which you'll write down both the sample ABCs and those that arise in your group.

Begin by posing a question to the group, for instance: "Three men in supposedly monogamous relationships catch their wives in bed with other men. The first rushes to the kitchen, grabs a butcher knife and stabs his wife and her lover to death. The second screams at them, but walks out, and later calls to coldly tell her that he's leaving her. The third walks out, calls and arranges to talk with her later, and when they do talk tells her that her that he loves her, but that if she's going to see other people he also wants to. Why did these men react so differently?"

Continue, "the answer is that they acted on different beliefs, some self-helping, some self-defeating. The first man believed that his wife *shouldn't* do such a thing (how dare she!), that the other man *shouldn't* have been with his wife, and that they both *deserved* to die, that they *must* die for doing it. The second man probably shared the first two beliefs, that they *shouldn't* have done it, but probably didn't share the belief that they *should* die—or at least he probably also held the self-helping belief that he didn't want to spend the rest of his life in jail for a rash act, even if he wanted to commit it. The third man might have held entirely different beliefs. He might have been unhappy with monogamy, viewed his wife's infidelity as not terribly important, and in fact might have seen it as an opening to get something that he wanted—her, plus the opportunity to see other women (or men). The reason that these three men reacted in totally dissimilar ways to essentially the same event is that they held totally dissimilar *beliefs* about it. The first man's beliefs pushed him into becoming angry and murderously enraged. The second man's beliefs pushed him to become angry and withdrawn. And the third man's beliefs created little or no anger, and allowed him to use the triggering (activating) event to his own advantage.

"This is how emotions are generated according to REBT theory: There's a triggering (activating) event; our beliefs about the event kick in; and we experience emotional (and behavioral) consequences.

"This emotion-causing chain can be outlined as follows:

A (Activating event): The triggering event.

B (Belief[s]): What you tell yourself about A. The(se) belief(s) can be either self-helping or self-defeating, and are often so ingrained, so seemingly natural, that we don't even notice what we're telling ourselves.

C (Consequence): The emotions that stem from A and B.

"When B (one's belief about the activating event, A) is self-helping, the C (emotional and physical consequences) tends to be conducive to happiness, or at least to minimal emotional upset. But when the B (belief) is self-defeating, it often leads to considerable emotional upset, and often to rash, destructive acts.

"To cite an example, suppose that you were driving and someone swerved in front of you, causing you to slam on the brakes. The consequences could vary drastically, depending on your beliefs about the incident:

A: You're cut off and have to slam on the brakes.

B (self-helping belief): It's irritating, but there's nothing useful I can do about it, so I'd best let it go rather than stew about it. It's a good thing I'm a defensive driver.

C: You calm down, feel proud of your driving abilities, continue on your way, and are quickly thinking of more pleasant things.

Or

A: You're cut off and have to slam on the brakes.

B (self-defeating belief): What a jerk! He *shouldn't* have done that! He *deserves* to be beaten to a pulp for doing it!

C: You work yourself into a rage, begin driving recklessly to catch him, and, quite possibly, are arrested for speeding or reckless driving; or, if you catch him, you assault him, and, again quite possibly, you're shot or stabbed, beaten to a pulp, or are arrested.

"One tipoff to self-defeating beliefs is that they almost always trigger unpleasant emotional consequences—anger, rage, guilt, shame, self-loathing, or depression (and, often, self-defeating behavior as well). When these emotions surface, it's always a good idea to look at what the triggering event is (this is almost always obvious) and what you're telling yourself about it (in other words, your beliefs)."

(This can be done quite fruitfully in groups, and it is in fact a mainstay of one of the modern [non-12-step] alcohol recovery groups, SMART Recovery. The procedure is simple: just take a problem that has arisen for one member of the group, and put the ABCs of the problem down on a blackboard.)

Going on, you could tell the group, "Let's add a 'D' (Disputation of the self-defeating belief) and an 'E' (Effective new belief). Continuing with our example, the 'D' and 'E' could be:

D: Why *shouldn't* he have done that? Everyone screws up sometimes. Does everyone deserve to be beaten to a pulp when they screw up? And who am I to say that someone *deserves* a beating?

E: The guy was driving like a jerk, but I have more pleasant things to do than to work myself into a rage.

"So, now that we understand the ABC process, does anyone here have something that they found upsetting or that they would like to work on?" If no one comes forward, ask if anyone in the group has felt very angry, bad about themselves, or has had any other very unpleasant emotions recently, and then go on from there, focusing on the negative feelings (C), the activating event(s) (A), and the belief (s) (B) that caused the unpleasant emotional consequences (C).

Note: One very good thing about this exercise is that it can take as little as 10 minutes out of a session, or it can easily, and productively, take up an entire session. A final note is that if you want the people in your group to fully understand this exercise (and thus their own emotions) and to make good use of the ABC process, it's a wise idea to devote at least some time to it during several consecutive sessions, and to stress that it's primarily a *written* procedure.

True or False?

Size: 5 to 25.

Time: 60 to 90 minutes.

Stage: Intermediate or advanced, though beginning groups could find this exercise helpful after a few meetings.

Remarks: This exercise introduces an element of fun while members get a chance at self-regulated levels of disclosure.

Explain that each group member will have the opportunity to be the focus of attention at least once, and likely more than once. Next, choose a member, or start yourself, and proceed in turn as follows: Each person makes three statements about him or herself—two true and one false. Following this, the rest of the group attempts, through open discussion, followed by a show of hands, to decide which statement is false. Then, the individual who made the statements reveals which of them was the lie. Allow no more than five minutes per person (that is, per every person's statements) for discussion. Proceed in turn, or randomly, until everyone in the group has made their three statements; then end the exercise or do another round.

Note: A variation on this game is to express two lies and one truth.

I Love Everybody Who

Size: 7 to 20.

Time: 45 to 90 minutes.

Stage: Intermediate.

Contraindications: A high level of distrust or antagonism between group members.

Remarks: This game can be a lot of fun. It helps people to loosen up, and once caught up in it many people will reveal things that they'd normally keep hidden. Thus, it's very useful in establishing a good comfort level in a group, and it's also a good way for group members to get to know each other quickly. It should be played outdoors or in a large, uncluttered room. This game is best played in a group that has been meeting for at least a few weeks and whose members feel comfortable with each other. The only real drawback is that you can only play this game once or twice in any group; after that it gets boring if the same people participate.

Count the number of people playing this game and set out, in a wide circle, that number of flat, nonslippery things to stand on—we recommend rubber place mats—minus one. (E.g., if you have 11 people playing the game, set out 10 pieces evenly in a circle at least 15 feet wide). Have everyone else stand on one of the flat pieces, and explain the exercise as follows: "The purpose of this game is to get better acquainted, to let us know more about each other. The way it works is that the person standing in the center of the circle will reveal something about himself or herself by saying, "I love everybody in this group who . . ." And the statement that they make must apply to themselves. So, if you're in the center and say, "I love everybody in this group who's had athlete's foot," you yourself must have had athlete's foot. Everyone whom the statement applies to, including the speaker, must attempt to move to a vacant spot—but not their own spot or the one next to it, unless only one other person in the circle moves. Whoever is left without a spot goes to the center and makes the next statement. Any questions? OK, let's start." Then move to the center of the circle and reveal something embarrassing about yourself, such as, "I love everybody in this group who has ever contracted a sexually transmitted disease."

Note: It is possible to use armless chairs in this exercise, but it's not a good idea to do so. People often get carried away in this exercise, and damage to chairs and injuries to participants are possible if chairs are used, so we strongly recommend the use of rubber place mats instead of chairs.

Role Reversal Dating

Size: 10 or more, with, preferably close to a balance in the numbers of men and women.

Time: 3 to 4 hours.

Stage: Beginning and intermediate groups.

Remarks: This exercise is written for heterosexual groups, although, obviously, it can easily be adapted for bisexual or gay groups. This intimacy-building exercise is actually more suited to retreats, workshops, and to previously agreed-to, longer-than-normal group meetings than it is to normal-length group meetings. It's a good exercise for a fairly new group, but should be done only after the group has met at least two or three times, so that the group's members have some sense of each other.

After this exercise is over, it's helpful for the men and women to meet again separately to discuss their reactions to it. This is especially useful given that this exercise involves role reversal, with the women doing the asking and facing possible rejection, and the men having to passively wait instead of initiating contact. Thus both men and women get a taste of the unpalatable aspects of the opposite sex's "normal" role in dating.

Of course, it's possible to do this exercise with the men doing the asking and the women doing the accepting or rejecting, but this version of the exercise is probably less valuable than the one involving role reversal.

This exercise flows best if the "dates" are scheduled at half-hour or hour intervals, with all "dates" being the same length.

Have the men and women meet separately, and have the individual women write out invitations to individual men to do anything that the women desire for one hour. The women will then read their invitations out loud and let each other know to which men they're directed. (The invitations could range from asking to get together for a walk, to asking to have sex.)

A go-between will then deliver the invitations to the men, who will then read their invitations out loud, and who will have the option of accepting, declining, or suggesting an alternative. The men will then write out their replies and propose times for their "dates" with the various women, and the go-between will deliver their responses to the women, who will schedule and write down the actual times and will accept or reject in writing any alternatives that the men proposed. The go-between will then deliver the written times to the men, plus any acceptances or rejections of proposed alternatives. The "dates" begin 15 minutes after the replies are sent. (It's helpful to use a blackboard or large drawing pad, in both the men's and women's groups, on which to post the times of the dates, in order to avoid confusion during this scheduling process. Use a grid format, with [for the men's group] the men's names running down the left side and the time marked at half-hour or hour intervals along the top. The women's group would use a similar grid, but with their own names running down the side.)

Following conclusion of the dates, have the men and women meet separately to discuss their experiences, and their reactions to those experiences.

Shame-Attacking Exercises

Size: Any number.

Time: Any duration, though usually short.

Stage: Any stage, though better for intermediate or advanced groups.

Remarks: This is a variation on a standard Rational Emotive Behavior Therapy (REBT) exercise. It can be done as either an individual or a group exercise. Its purpose is to show individuals that their phobias and shame are largely of their own manufacture, and in many cases are groundless. To put it another way, this exercise is designed to show that most people are so self-preoccupied that they don't care what you do as long as it doesn't directly affect them. (Of course, the sexually repressed tend to be hypersensitive to the sexual behavior of others, so this exercise normally excludes sexual expression—at least in public places.)

Individual Exercise: This is the normal REBT form of this exercise. In it, in a public setting, an individual performs some action which he or she finds embarrassing. The only limitations are that the action be nonthreatening and nonharmful to self and others, that it not lead to its performer being assaulted or arrested, and that you do it in a place where no one is likely to recognize you. The two classical suggestions for this exercise are to board a bus or streetcar and call out the stops, or to put a banana on a leash and walk it as if it were a dog. But the variations are endless. To cite a couple of examples, one very self-conscious man who hated calling attention to himself started wearing dashikis and Hawaiian shirts in place of his normal drab clothing—and found that he liked it. Another man walked up to a number of total strangers, pulled back his hair from his forehead, and asked them if they thought he was going bald.

Group Exercise: Assign this exercise at the session before it's to take place. An effective way of doing this is to take one (or two or three) participants aside privately and instruct them to do or say something at the next meeting that they would be embarrassed to do or say, but with the precaution that it be nonthreatening and nonharmful. In many cases it's a good idea to suggest actions that you know that the person will find embarrassing, especially actions that the person might find enjoyable if they overcame their embarrassment. A good example is to instruct an individual with a phobia about singing to sing a song at the next meeting. One reason for assigning the shame-attacking exercise at a prior meeting is that it gives members at least several days to think about it, and thus increases the sense of dread before the exercise, and the feeling of relief after it's performed. This exercise can be quite liberating, and it can (in various forms) be performed many times. One useful variation, with shy individuals, is to have the person who's "it" publicly declare to someone else in the group that s/he finds him or her attractive.

Feedback

Size: 3 to 20.
Time: 60 to 90 minutes.
Stage: Intermediate or advanced.
Remarks: There are a number of group feedback processes.
It helps to remember that they can be tricky, and that set-up and timing are usually crucial when using them. Feedback processes are touchy because they take the focus of a group out of the abstract, or out of impersonal questions, and move it to matters of personal import. For example, it is one thing to say, "My favorite color is red; I believe in socialism; I think . . . is a good choice for mayor"; etc., and quite another to say, "I like . . . about you; I didn't like it when (group member) did such and such; I don't like being around so-and-so." These are personally meaningful and revealing statements. Such statements help to clarify where members stand in relation to the group and to each other, and can lead to real intimacy. Feedback processes can be difficult, but they often add depth to a group. When a person speaks his or her "truth," other members learn about that person, and may put aside misperceptions about him or her. Feedback is a form of sharing of oneself, of intimacy, if you will.

The following feedback exercise can be done in one, two, or three stages depending upon the nature of the group and the desired effect—that is, how deep you want to go.

Stage 1

Have every group member write down the name(s) of one or two other group member(s) that they are attracted to and/or want to spend more time with. This becomes their "A" list. Next, have them list the one person in the group that they are least attracted to. This becomes their "B " list. After this, give everyone a few minutes to decide what they like and what they dislike about the people they've listed. For example, in the case of those they're attracted to, is it spontaneity, dependability, physical attractiveness, intelligence, sense of humor, optimism, etc.? Group members should then write these things down next to the names on their lists. By doing this, individuals should become more aware of what they find attractive and unattractive in others. (This can be taken a step further if individuals decide to explore why they find certain traits attractive and others unattractive, and which traits they find particularly significant. If several people—let alone all group members—did this, it would take too much group time, so this is best done as a written, homework exercise, which can be fruitfully discussed at the next meeting.)

After everyone has completed the above steps, have them share in turn who was on their "A" list, and the traits and characteristics on the "A" and "B" lists. The exercise can stop here or proceed to a deeper level.

Stage 2

Check with the group members to see if they want to go to the next level, that is, to discuss and process their reactions to stage one of this exercise. If the majority decide to proceed, continue by questioning all of the group's members in turn.

Useful questions include :

- How did it feel to be on someone's "A" list?
- How did it feel to not be mentioned on someone's "A" list?
- Did you have a reaction to being on someone's "A" list who you didn't mention on your "A" list?
- Did you have a reaction to not being on someone's "A" list who you had put on yours?
- What do your reactions tell you about yourself?
- Were you surprised by any revelations?
- Did these disclosures conform to your perceptions about other group members or not, that is, to who likes who?

Stage 3

After the stage-two discussion takes place, this feedback exercise can proceed to an even deeper level by having everyone reveal who was on their "B" list. (But this step is best done only if *all* members agree to it.) It may be helpful to start off by asking a series of questions, such as the following:

- What are you most afraid of in this exercise?
- What if you heard your name more than once on "B" lists?
- What would be the most difficult thing for you to deal with, and why would it be difficult?

Even if the group members decide not to reveal their "B" list names, this discussion helps to reveal more about each individual. And if they agree to go on, continue by utilizing questions based on those in Stage 2, but substituting "B list" for "A list." In this stage, it's essential that discussion be limited to what members have learned about *themselves* and about *their own* reactions. As with most other difficult exercises, it's good to end this phase of the feedback exercise with a round of appreciations (see pp. 27–28).

Advanced Feedback

Size: 4 to 15.

Time: 60 to 90 minutes.

Stage: Advanced.

Remarks: We recommend this exercise only for groups that have been meeting for some time, and whose members have had a number of interactions with one another, both inside and outside the group. We do *not* recommend this exercise for beginning groups. Good facilitation is essential to the success of this exercise.

This is *not* a blaming exercise. Its purpose is to help individuals deepen their awareness of the part that they play in perpetuating negative situations—to discover and acknowledge their trigger points, and to acknowledge their feelings and behaviors after being triggered.

Begin by asking the group members to pay full attention to the exercise and not to engage in private conversations during it. Then, give all members a copy of the following feedback form and encourage them to look around the room and recall both positive and negative reactions they have had to other group members. (Either photocopy the following directly from this book or, better, reformat it and reproduce it on larger sheets of paper with plenty of blank space for members to write in names, situations, etc.)

● I had a positive/negative perception of you (name) when (state objective occurrence or situation). I perceived you to be (characteristic—positive example: generous, warm, capable, considerate, caring, intelligent, trustworthy, honest, etc.; negative example: cold, selfish, judgmental, aggressive, domineering, insensitive, inconsiderate, abandoning, etc.).

• I reacted to you by (state action — positive example: talking to you, trusting you, calling you, spending time with you, etc.; negative example: withdrawing, blaming you, judging you, attempting to prove you wrong, avoiding you, trying to hurt you, etc).

• I am/am not still feeling this positivity/negativity toward you.

Next, explore the difference between objective and subjective reality with the group. Use examples, either culled from the group or that you come up with yourself. Emphasize that one's *interpretation* of things is *not* the same as the things themselves.

To cite an example, say that one group member felt that another member had been cold and arrogant by not returning a greeting. The objective part of this is that the person didn't return the greeting. The subjective part is the interpretation that he or she was being cold and arrogant. Point out that the subjective interpretation might not be accurate, because the person who didn't respond might not have seen or heard the other person, or might have been so lost in thought that they simply didn't notice the greeting; and also point out that the best way to check on the accuracy of the subjective interpretation is to simply ask the person who didn't respond why they didn't do it.

Next, ask each person in the group to take a turn in front of the group expressing their positive perception of and reaction to another group member. After they do this, the person they reacted to may only say, "Thank you." Continue until all members have given and received positive feedback.

As soon as the positive-feedback portion of this exercise is over, ask each person in the group to take a turn in front of the group expressing their negative perception of and reaction to another group member. After they do this, the person they reacted to can only say, "Thank you." Continue until all members have given and received negative feedback.

Although there will be great desire for immediate discussion of this exercise, do not allow it. In order to help your group members accept this, point out that the purpose of this exercise is to allow individuals to note, and think about, their trigger points, and their reactions to being triggered. Continue by stating that the group will discuss this exercise at its next meeting, but that discussion will be limited to what members learned about *themselves*.

This can be a very difficult process, so it's a good idea to conclude this exercise with a round of appreciations (see pp. 27–28).

Ping-Pong Questions

Size: 4 to 15.
Time: 60 to 90 minutes.
Stage: Advanced.
Contraindications: Low trust level.
Remarks: Helpful in breaking through the "niceness" barrier. It's a good idea to keep close track of time and to end this exercise at a predetermined time. As well, it's a good idea to begin with some type of intimacy- or trust-building exercise, and to end with a round of appreciations.

Explain the game as follows: "Tonight, we're going to ask each other a lot of questions. The purpose of this is to help us get to know each other better, and to become more direct in our dealings with each other. The way this works is that one person starts by asking someone else something they'd normally be too embarrassed or too afraid to ask, or that they think would embarrass the person being asked, but that they genuinely want to know. The person being asked doesn't have to answer the question unless they want to, but they do have to ask someone else a potentially embarrassing question. Then that person has to ask someone else an embarrassing question. The only limit to what you can ask is that your questions be about things that you genuinely want to know. If you feel uncomfortable when you think of a question for someone (at least ones for which you genuinely want to know the answer), it's probably a good sign that you should ask it. Does everybody understand? Good. This exercise will take an hour. Let's start now."

There are two ways to start. One is to ask a very pointed question to someone you think will handle it well, and you're off and running. (For instance, if you had a bisexual person in the group, who was in a monogamous relationship, you could ask him or her, "You're bisexual, but you're in a monogamous relationship. Is that what you really want? And if not, why are you doing it?") A second way, that we recommend, is to have someone else in the group ask you a thorny question. If the question isn't pointed enough, direct the questioner to ask a harder question—one that they think might embarrass you—and go on from there.

After you've finished, take a few minutes for the group to discuss the exercise and to talk about what came up for everyone individually during it.

As with meetings featuring other difficult exercises, it's a good idea to end any meeting where this exercise is used with a round of appreciations (see pp. 27–28).

Secrets & Revelations

Size: 5 to 20.
Time: 2 to 3 hours.
Stage: Intermediate and advanced.
Remarks: This exercise is very intense and is best done in groups that have been meeting for at least a couple of months and in which some trust is already established. For a group of 15 using 3 questions, this exercise should take about 2½ hours. (With groups larger than 15, it's necessary to reduce the number of questions from 3 to 2.) If you have regularly scheduled meetings, this exercise should be announced at the meeting prior to the one in which it will take place, in order to allow those with high levels of fear or distrust to avoid participating in it.

First announce, "This exercise will deal with our deepest, most painful secrets, and what we reveal here will go no farther than this room. If you do not want to participate in this exercise or do not agree to keep everything revealed here confidential, please go to the next room where a discussion group will be held by those who do not wish to participate. Does everyone agree not to reveal to others what they hear here today?" (A good topic for those who opt out—if anyone does—is why they opted out.)

Next, have the group sit in a circle. Then give everyone three identical pieces of blank paper (at least half the size of a normal 8½"x11" sheet) and identical writing implements. Tell them, "Please write down your three deepest, darkest secrets, one secret per sheet of paper, and write on only one side of the paper. These secrets should be the ones that you're most ashamed of, the ones that you would feel the most embarrassed about revealing to the group. When you've written down your secrets, please fold your papers in half and put them on the pile in the center of the circle." After a pause, say, "At the end of this exercise, if everyone agrees, we'll reveal what our secrets are. If anyone doesn't want to, no one will reveal their secrets." Allow 10 to 15 minutes for people to write down their secrets.

Then, thoroughly shuffle the papers. After they're shuffled, have everyone in the group take three papers at random from the pile. (It doesn't matter if someone pulls one or two of their own papers.) Next, tell them, "We'll go around in a circle reading these secrets out loud, one at a time. After you read a secret, react to that revelation *as if you had written it.* Say how having that secret makes you feel." Then add, "After each secret is read, we'll let two people briefly tell us their reactions to it." (If the group is small, three reactions would be OK—the purpose of restricting the number of spoken reactions is to conserve time. Also, the spoken reactions should be brief—no more than 30 seconds each—and it's good to get reactions from different people rather than the same people after every revealed secret; if one or a few people attempt to always state their reactions, make a point of not choosing them and instead ask silent members for their reactions.)

Start by reading one of the secrets you hold in your hand and, putting yourself in the place of the person who wrote it, say how having that secret makes you feel. Then ask, "Does anybody want to share how they felt hearing this secret?" If more than two people want to share, choose which two will do it, and listen to their reactions. Then ask the person on your left or right to read next, and continue going around in a circle until all of the secrets have been read and the reactions to them have been heard. Then, go around in a circle one more time taking up to one minute each (if the group is large) or two minutes each (if the group is small), and have everyone say how they felt hearing their own secrets read and the reactions to them (but instruct them not to reveal their own secrets), and how they felt hearing other individuals' secrets.

After this round is completed, ask, "Is it OK with everyone if we reveal our secrets now?" If anyone objects, ask why, and ask if there's anything the group can do to help them feel safe enough to reveal their secrets. If anyone seems sure that they don't want to reveal theirs, ask them why again, and if there's anything anyone can do to help them feel safe enough to do it. If they persist in saying "no," respect it and end the exercise. If they seem ambivalent, work with them until they resolve the matter. If they're still ambivalent after 10 or 15 minutes of discussion, direct them to make a decision. If they refuse to decide, take it as a "no."

If people are OK about revealing their secrets, go first yourself, and then continue around in a circle, taking two minutes (if the group is large) to five minutes (if the group is small) per person to reveal your secrets and state your feelings. Within the per-person time limit, questions and comments are OK after a person has finished revealing their secrets and stating their feelings.

Finally, have everyone walk outside and form a circle, place the papers in the center of the circle, and burn them. (If it's raining, tearing the papers up into tiny bits indoors will serve the same purpose as burning them.) Close with a group hug and by thanking everyone, during the hug, for having the courage to participate in this exercise.